Touching

Lillian Wright

RSVP
RAINTREE
STECK-VAUGHN
P U B L I S H E R S
The Steck-Vaughn Company

Austin, Texas

Series Editor: Pippa Pollard
Science Editor: Kim Merlino
Design: Sally Boothroyd
Project Manager: Julie Klaus
Electronic Production:
   Scott Melcer
Artwork: Mainline Design
Cover Art: Mainline Design

Library of Congress Cataloging-in-Publication Data
Wright, Lillian.
      Touching /Lillian Wright.
         p.   cm. — (First starts)
      Includes index.
      ISBN 0-8114-5517-3
      1. Touch — Juvenile literature.
[1. Touch.   2. Senses and sensation.]   I. Title.   II. Series.
QP451.W75 1995
612.8'8—dc20   94-12939
                                  CIP
                                  AC

Printed and bound in the United States

1 2 3 4 5 6 7 8 9 0 LB 98 97 96 95 94

Contents

What Is Touch?

Touch is one of our five senses. The others are seeing, hearing, smelling, and tasting. We can close our eyes and cover our ears. But we cannot "turn off" our sense of touch. Our skin can feel all kinds of touches—pressure, texture, heat, cold, and pain.

▽ We use our sense of touch to learn more about the world around us.

3

Talking About Touch

When we touch things, they often feel very different. We have many words to describe these feelings, like sharp, soft, smooth, spongy, slippery, silky, bumpy, scratchy, and prickly. How many more can you think of? We may like the feel of one thing but dislike another.

▷ Think of all the different objects you touch every day. How would you describe the way they feel?

▷ Many people enjoy touching and stroking the soft fur of an animal. Would you like to stroke a rough brick this way?

▷ Sand can feel dry and almost silky. Sometimes it feels wet and scratchy.

How Does Touch Work?

Inside our skin we have millions of tiny **touch sensors** that send signals to our **brain**. There are different kinds of touch sensors. Some can tell if an object is hot or cold. Other sensors tell our brain about pressure. Still different ones tell about pain. Some sensors can tell us about more than one feeling. They help to save our body from injury and harm.

▷ Beneath the outer layer of our skin lie different types of touch sensors. Each one sends its own signals to your brain.

▽ This is a touch sensor. It has been magnified many times.

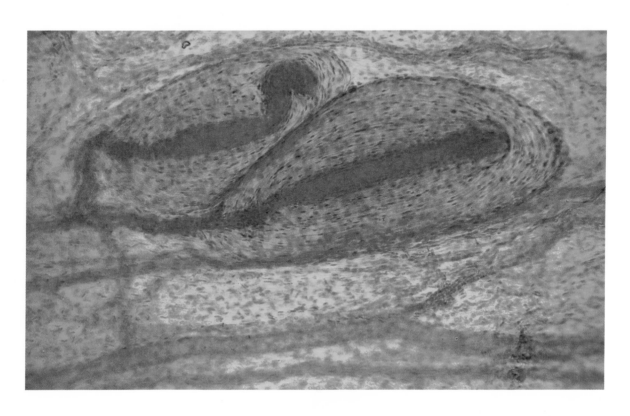

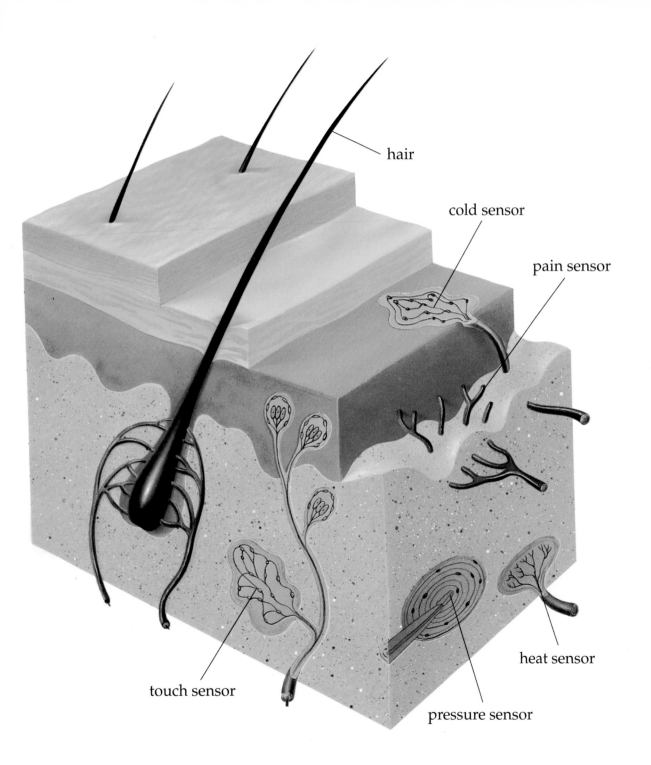

hair

cold sensor

pain sensor

touch sensor

pressure sensor

heat sensor

7

How Sensitive Are You to Touch?

Our skin is not equally sensitive to touch all over. Our lips are more sensitive to touch than our back is. Our eyes are more sensitive than our legs. This is because there are more touch sensors packed together in the skin of our lips and eyes than in our back or legs. These touch sensors are often found in groups. The tip of the tongue has the most touch sensors.

▽ Animals also have parts of their bodies that are particularly sensitive to touch. A cat's whiskers are important. They extend the cat's sense of touch beyond its body.

▷ You can test how sensitive you are to touch at different points on your body.

Tie two pencils together. Ask a friend to touch you gently with the points on your back and on the tips of your fingers. Can you feel both points on your back? Can you feel both points on your fingers?

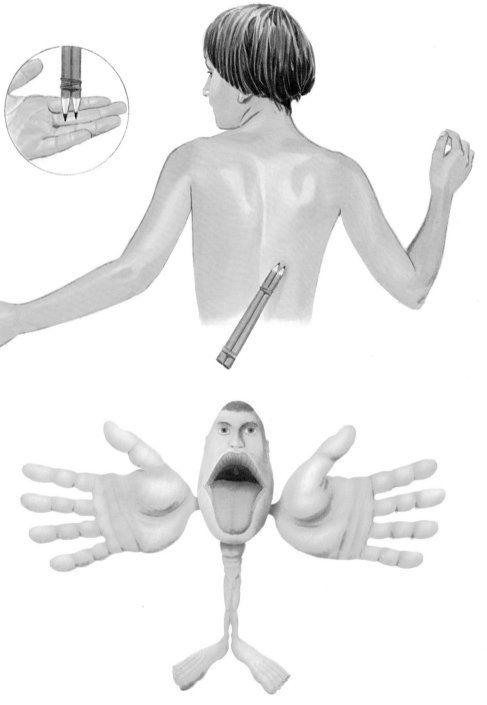

▷ This drawing shows what you would look like if each part of your body was drawn in proportion to how sensitive it is to touch. So parts of your body with a lot of touch sensors, such as lips and fingertips, are drawn very large.

Using Our Hands

There are more touch sensors in our fingertips than in most other parts of our body. We normally use our fingertips to feel something. Using our wrists, knuckles, or the back of our hands would not tell us as much. Those parts have fewer touch sensors. Touch sensors only last a short time. They are constantly being replaced, changing their position in our skin.

▽ We can see what color the glass is and what it contains. But it is our fingertips that tell us the glass feels cold and hard.

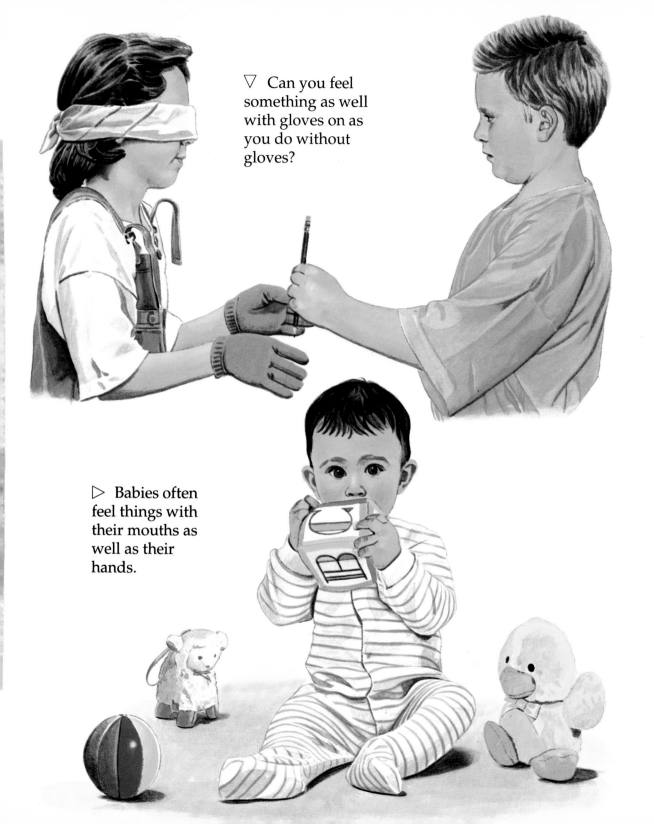

▽ Can you feel something as well with gloves on as you do without gloves?

▷ Babies often feel things with their mouths as well as their hands.

Fingertips and Fingernails

Our fingernails help our sense of touch. They form a stiff pad behind our sensitive fingertips. This gives each fingertip support as we press and poke things. Without fingernails, the flesh on our fingertips would bend back. Then fewer sensors would be **stimulated**.

▷ Our fingernails help our fingertips feel a light touch. A blind person can "read" the raised dots of a Braille book with his or her fingertips.

▷ It does not hurt to cut your nails because they are made of a dead substance called keratin. Nails do not contain touch sensors.

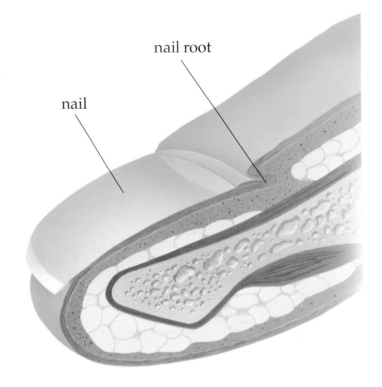

nail root

nail

Reflex Action

Our sense of touch helps to keep us safe. If we touch something very hot, our body moves away quickly. Our reaction is so quick that we do not choose to move away. Our nerves in the spinal cord tell the body directly. This keeps us from being badly hurt. This quick response to touch is called a **reflex action**.

▷ Dust or dirt can irritate the nose. Sneezing is a reflex action that gets rid of dust or dirt in the nose.

▷ If something touches your eye or the skin around it, you blink right away to protect your delicate eye. This is a reflex action.

Hot and Cold

Some sensors in our skin can feel whether it is hot or cold. They help us know when there is a change in temperature. This is important because our body must not get too hot or too cold. If our skin gets too warm, it sends messages to the brain. The brain then tells the body to sweat to help it cool off.

▷ If the body gets too cold, our cold sensors alert the brain. Often this results in shivering or goose bumps.

▽ When our body starts to get too warm, we may feel flushed and start to sweat.

▽ Our body is not equally
sensitive to heat and cold all
over. Try testing your elbow,
toe, and finger in a bowl of
warm water. Which makes
the water feel the warmest?

Feeling Pain

We can feel a number of different kinds of pain. If an insect stings or a plant pricks us, our skin may become sore and itchy. When a hard ball hits our leg, we may feel a sharp pain. If we fall and twist our ankle, it may throb and ache. Pain is a very important warning sign that our body may be damaged.

▽ A bruise is an injury caused by bleeding under the skin. A hard blow breaks the blood vessels and blood leaks into the area around it. This causes painful pressure on the touch sensors in the skin.

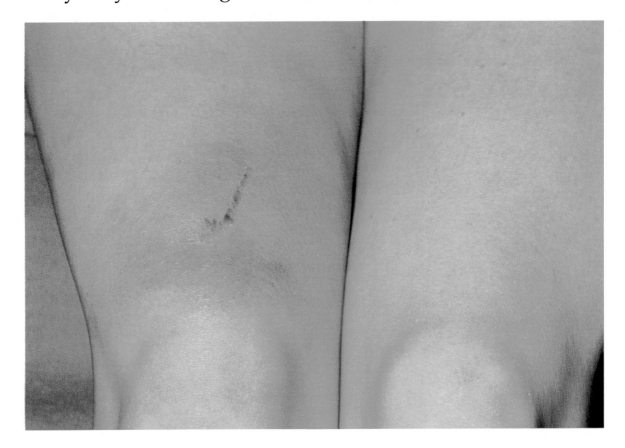

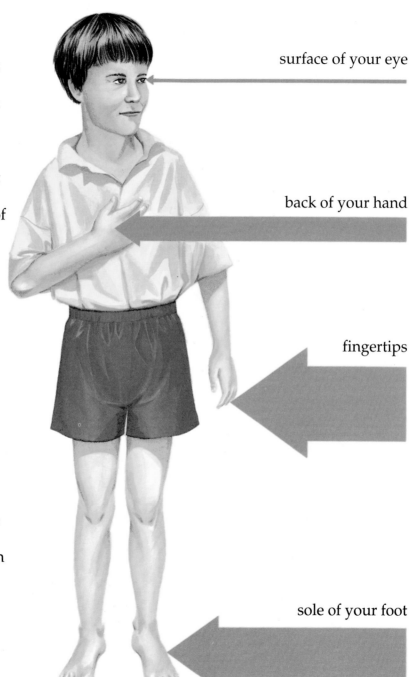

▷ The touch sensors that respond to pain are not spread out evenly over the body. It takes a lot of pressure to feel pain in the tips of our fingers, but very little to feel it in our eye. That is why just a speck of dirt in the eye can make it sore.

surface of your eye

back of your hand

fingertips

▷ In this picture, the larger the colored arrow, the more pressure it takes to cause pain in that part of the body.

sole of your foot

Itches and Tickles

When we put on new clothes, they sometimes tickle or make us feel itchy. At first, they send strong signals to our brain. But a little at a time the sensors in the skin get so used to the feeling that the signal fades. Then we no longer notice it.

▷ Tickling our skin excites the touch sensors and can really make us laugh!

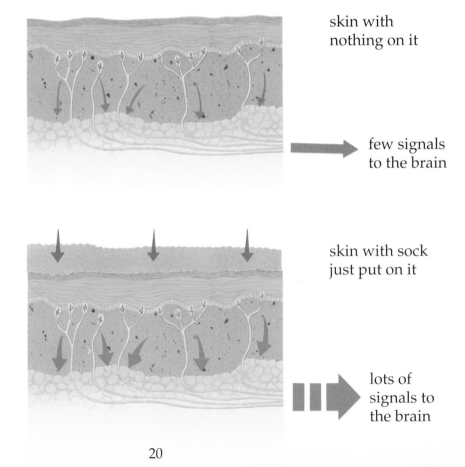

skin with nothing on it

few signals to the brain

▷ When you put clothes on your skin, they send strong signals to your brain at first. But the signals fade when you have gotten used to having the clothes on.

skin with sock just put on it

lots of signals to the brain

Feelings Inside

Our senses work inside our body, too. If something gets stuck in your throat, the sensors there tell your brain. Then you cough to try to move and swallow it. Sometimes we cough because sensors tell the brain there is something harmful in the lungs. There are also sensors that tell us when we need to drink fluids. Sensors even tell us when we are hungry.

▷ Sensors inside our stomachs tell us when we have eaten enough and are full.

▽ After running we may feel our heart pounding. We may also feel thirsty.

Balancing

Our sense of balance is similar to our sense of touch. We need our sense of balance to keep standing upright and to perform many movements. Inside our ears are three bony tubes or canals. These are called **semicircular canals**. They have nothing to do with hearing. They can tell us which way our head is moving. They can also tell us the position of our head.

▽ This gymnast has to practice to achieve such good balance.

▽ Liquid inside our semicircular canals moves as we do. Tiny hairs that are connected to sensory cells pick up the inner movement. They send signals to the brain about the position of our head.

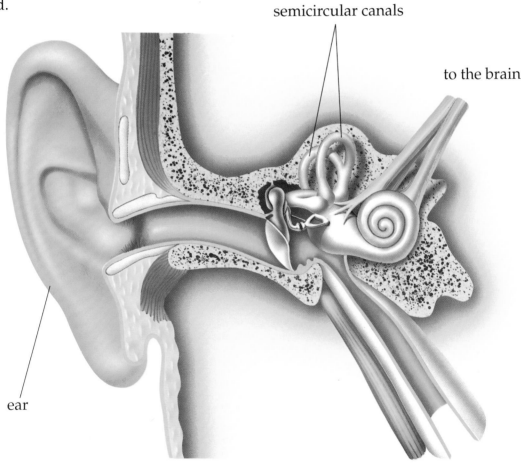

semicircular canals

to the brain

ear

No Feeling

At the dentist's office we may sometimes be given an injection. This stops us from feeling any pain and makes our mouth feel numb. This way the dentist can work on our teeth without hurting us. Slowly, the injection wears off and feeling comes back again. Sometimes in an accident or because of an illness a nerve is damaged or cut. This could mean that we may not be able to feel pain, heat, or cold anymore.

▷ When someone has an operation they are given an anesthetic to keep them from feeling any pain.

▽ There are no nerves in our nails or in our hair. This is because they are made of a dead substance called keratin. It does not hurt to cut them.

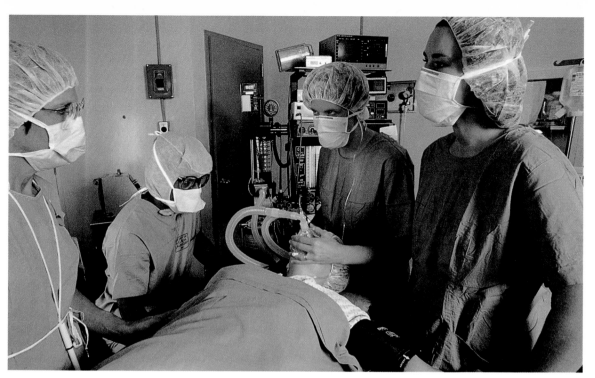

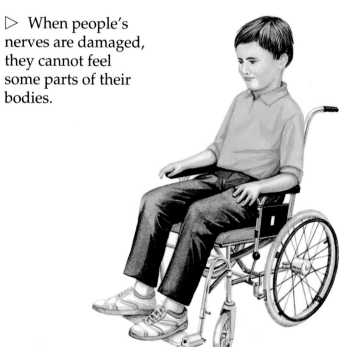

▷ When people's nerves are damaged, they cannot feel some parts of their bodies.

Using Touch

We use our sense of touch for many things. Pain is an unpleasant feeling, but it protects our body from harm. Other feelings, such as the warm sun on our skin, are much more pleasant. Our sense of touch helps us to let other people know what we feel about them. It is another important way of **communicating** our feelings to people. Some people need to use their sense of touch for their work.

▷ A hug or a kiss from a child to a parent shows a feeling of love.

▷ Although a carpenter may not see that the wood is smooth, he can feel it.

Things to Do

- Put on a blindfold. Can you tell who is a friend, parent, or child by touch alone?

- Stand on one leg and hold your other leg behind you. Start leaning forward. Can you tell right away when you have gone as far as you can without falling over? Practice and see if you can improve you sense of balance.

- Work with a friend. Each of you makes a list of objects you enjoy touching. Make another list of objects that you don't like to touch. Is your list the same as your friend's? Do you think there are things we all like to touch?

Useful Addresses:

Liberty Science Center
Attn: Elizabeth Graham
251 Phillip Street
Jersey City, NJ 07305-4699

Ontario Science Centre
770 Don Mills Road
Toronto
Ontario, Canada M3C1T3

Glossary

anesthetic A substance that causes loss of feeling in all or part of our body. Dentists and surgeons use anesthetics so that patients do not feel any pain.

Braille A system of writing and printing for blind people, made of clusters of raised dots representing numbers and letters. These raised dots are "read" by touching them lightly.

brain The organ protected by our skull that receives messages from the nerves of our body. The brain "tells" us what is going on around us.

communicating Giving information about something.

efficient Able to produce an effect without wasting time or energy.

goose bumps Tiny raised bumps on our skin that make it look like a plucked chicken. These are caused by cold or sometimes by fear.

nerve A pathway inside our bodies that carries messages between all parts of our body and our brain.

reflex action A quick automatic action that takes place when some nerve cells are stimulated.

semicircular canals A structure shaped like a half circle inside our ears. These help us keep our sense of balance.

stimulated Pushed into action.

Index

Photographic credits: Alex Bartel/Science Photo Library 3; Martin Dohrn/Science Photo Library 17; Chris Fairclough Colour Library 23, 24; Eric Grave/Science Photo Library 6; Ken Lax/Science Photo Library 15; Dr P. Marazzi/Science Photo Library 18; Will & Deni McIntyre/Science Photo Library 13, 26; Gavin Wickham/Eye Ubiquitous 8; ZEFA 5, 21, 29.